John Taylor
Lord Taylor of Warwick
A PROFILE

Onyekachi Wambu
illustrated by Gillian Hunt

Tamarind Ltd

OTHER BOOKS IN THE
Black Profiles Series

BENJAMIN ZEPHANIAH
DR SAMANTHA TROSS
MALORIE BLACKMAN
BARONESS SCOTLAND OF ASTHAL
JIM BRATHWAITE

Published by Tamarind Ltd 2000
PO Box 52, Northwood
Middlesex HA6 1UN, UK

Text © Onyekachi Wambu
Illustrations © Gillian Hunt
Series editor: Simona Sideri

ISBN 1-870516-50-8

All rights reserved.
No part of this publication may be reproduced, stored in a retrieval system,
or transmitted, in any form, or by any means, electrical, mechanical, photocopying,
recording or otherwise without the prior permission
of the publishers.

Printed in Singapore

Contents

1 IN COURT 1
2 ALL IN A DAY'S WORK 5
3 DIFFICULT TIMES 9
4 SCHOOL DAYS 11
5 TO BE OR NOT TO BE 13
6 FOOTBALL AND THE FUTURE 16
7 GROWN-UP CHOICES 18
8 UNIVERSITY DAYS 20
9 A CAPTIVE AUDIENCE 23
10 GOING INTO POLITICS 26
11 1992 AND ALL THAT 30
12 STANDING FOR PARLIAMENT 32
13 ELECTION DAY 36
14 BECOMING A LORD 38

LORD TAYLOR'S ACHIEVEMENTS 42

CHAPTER ONE

In Court

ONE DAY IN 1996, JOHN TAYLOR sat in a cold, crowded courtroom in Birmingham. Beside him, tense and quiet, sat his client, Dean Jones. John, the only black person in the large courtroom, was a barrister, and for the last two hours, he had been trying to save an innocent man from prison.

John's next few words would decide whether Dean would spend the next five years in jail, or whether he would go free.

Dean was accused of robbing a post office. The woman behind the counter had been terrified by a sinister looking gunman in a stocking mask who had screamed at her to hand over the cash. That woman was now standing in the witness box. She still seemed terrified.

John rose to question her.

"The person who robbed you," he asked kindly, "did he have an accent?"

"Yes, a Scottish one," replied the woman.

"A Scottish accent. Are you sure?" John asked.

"Yes, I'm positive!" she replied.

"So the person who robbed you had a Scottish accent?" John repeated.

"Yes, I'm positive!" she said again. "I have friends and family in Scotland and I've been there plenty of times," she added. "I know a Scottish accent when I hear it."

"Then my client, Dean Jones, is not the gunman who robbed you," said John.

Everyone stared at him, wondering how he could be so sure.

It soon became clear when Dean took the witness stand.

"Please tell the court your name and address, your place of work and type of work," said John.

Dean's hands were shaking. He was so scared he could barely look up, but he spoke loudly enough for everyone to hear. It immediately dawned on the whole courtroom that Dean Jones could not possibly be the gunman. His accent was unmistakable. But it wasn't Scottish – he spoke with a broad Cockney twang.

The judge dismissed the case.

"Thank you, sir, thank you," Dean said to John, as

he walked free. John had won another victory in court but there was no time for celebration. He jumped into a taxi and raced across Birmingham to catch a train back to London and prepare for his next case.

CHAPTER TWO
All in a Day's Work

THE NEXT DAY WAS VERY IMPORTANT for John. The Queen was opening Parliament and all the Lords and Ladies were there, dressed in their traditional robes.

In his office, John hoisted his heavy red and ermine knee length gown with its white fur collar onto his shoulders.

"Phew!" he said to himself. "If the room is warm, I'll be cooked to a frazzle."

For the very first time, John was taking part in the State Opening of Parliament as Lord John Taylor of Warwick.

As he took his seat with the rest of the peers, John looked up towards the public gallery and smiled at his mother. She smiled back proudly.

He then turned to listen to the Queen as she began to read out all the new laws that were going to be passed by the government in the coming year.

When the ceremony was over, John had a meeting at Number 10 Downing Street with the then Prime Minister, John Major.

One of John Taylor's duties, as a member of the House of Lords, was to give advice to the government on legal matters. The meeting went well. On his way out of the Prime Minister's Office, John checked his diary.

"Ah, this will be fun," he said to himself as he made his way back to his office. His next appointment was with a group of schoolchildren who were visiting the House of Lords.

Outside, the children gazed upwards as Big Ben struck the hour. John told them about a cell at the bottom of the clock tower where, in the past, unruly MPs were detained. The last person to be imprisoned there was Charles Bradlaugh, MP for Northampton. In 1880 he was put in the cell for refusing to take the oath of allegiance to Queen Victoria.

Inside, John gave the children a tour of the grand building. They saw the golden throne where the Queen sits during the State Opening of Parliament and the original death warrant of King Charles in the Royal Gallery.

One boy asked whether this beautiful old building was the one that Guy Fawkes tried to blow up. John explained that the present building was built in Victorian times. But it stands on the same site as the one that Guy Fawkes tried to blow up.

The children had plenty of questions, but in particular, they were curious about how John Taylor had become a Lord.

"Was your father a Lord?" asked one.

"Do you live in Warwick Castle with loads of butlers?" asked another.

John laughed. "No," he replied. "Far from it. My father was not a Lord, and I certainly don't live in a castle. I come from very humble beginnings…"

Chapter Three

Difficult Times

JOHN TAYLOR WAS BORN IN 1952, just outside Warwick, a town near Birmingham.

His parents were from Jamaica. John's father was hardworking and clever and had worked as an accountant. He loved to relax playing his favourite sport – cricket. He was an excellent batsman.

John's parents were happy in Jamaica, but poor. Jobs had become very scarce, so in 1950, along with hundreds of others, they had come to Britain, hoping to find work.

In England, the only job John's father was offered was sweeping floors in a factory. Finding a house for the family was worse. Many white people would not rent their houses to black people. Eventually, they found a small place to rent. They worked hard and saved hard. Two years after arriving in England, they had saved enough money for a down payment on their first home.

Soon after, John was born. They were delighted.

John's early childhood years were uneventful. His mother stayed at home to look after him. His father continued to go to work.

CHAPTER FOUR
School Days

IN 1957, JOHN TURNED FIVE YEARS OLD and started school at Moseley Church of England Primary School in Birmingham. Most of the time he was happy, but one group of children kept taunting him and calling him names.

"What shall I do?" John complained to his parents. "I feel like punching them really hard. Then maybe they'll stop."

"John," his mother told him, "don't even think of punching anyone, ever! You'll just get into big trouble! Some children can be very nasty. Just keep well away from them. They may learn to behave better one day."

By the end of his time there, John had made a small group of good friends at the school.

In 1963, when John was eleven years old, he passed the eleven plus examination and went to Moseley Grammar School in Birmingham.

He made some more good friends there. He was bright and he worked hard so he had good marks in most subjects.

John loved reading and for his twelfth birthday, his mother gave him a book about an American called Dr Martin Luther King. John read how badly black people were treated in America.

I have a dream that my four little children will one day live in a nation where they will be judged not by the colour of their skin, but by the content of their character...

He learned that some black children were stopped from getting a good education. He thought Martin Luther King was great because he helped people who were oppressed.

John's parents continued to encourage him to read and work hard at school because they believed that a good education was the best weapon against ignorance and unfair treatment.

Chapter Five

To Be or Not to Be

THE TIME CAME FOR CHOOSING CAREERS and a teacher asked John what he wanted to do when he left school.

"I want to be a lawyer," John replied. He was now thirteen years old.

"Why do you want to do law?" asked the teacher.

"I just want to. I think I'll like it," replied John.

The careers teacher frowned, shook his head and said, "I think you're too ambitious, my boy. There are other things you can do."

"But that's what I want to do," John insisted.

"I don't want to be negative John," said his teacher.

"But it's just that I haven't seen any black lawyers in England. Why not try something else?"

John walked home from school that day, sad and discouraged.

"Come here John," said his mother. "What's the matter?"

"You know I want to be a lawyer, Mum?" said John.

"Yes, I know," said his mother. "And...?"

"Well, I was talking about it with one of my teachers, and he says he's never seen a black lawyer... So I suppose that means I can't be one."

"John, listen to me," his mum said. "The fact that *he* has never seen any black lawyers does not mean that they don't exist. And what your teacher has seen and what he has not seen has got nothing to do with *you* and what *you* want to be! You can be anything, John. And if you want to change your mind and choose something else, you can! If no other black people have done it, then you can be the first. You can be a good role model. Everyone can then follow you!"

"Wow, Mum," said John and ran off before she could say another word.

The next day, walking down a school corridor, he passed the teacher who didn't think he could be a lawyer.

"I'll show you," muttered John, as they passed each other.

"What did you say lad?" asked the teacher.

"Nothing, sir" said John, and sprinted out into the playground.

CHAPTER SIX

Football and the Future

JOHN WAS REALLY KEEN TO BE A LAWYER, but it very nearly didn't happen at all. One of the reasons for this was that he fell in love… with football.

He was the Birmingham Schools' 100 metres sprint champion, so he was fast. That's why he was chosen to take part in the football trials for the Aston Villa Under Fourteens at Villa Park stadium.

On the day of the trials he was nervous. The first half of the game seemed to fly by in a blur. In the second half, John received a pass at the half way line. Moving like the wind he weaved in and out between the players, dribbling towards the penalty area. One of the defenders came at him with a flying tackle. John could see two other opposing players closing in. He swung his right foot without even looking at the goal. The ball knifed its way through the defence into the top far left hand corner of the goal. A roar went up from the crowd.

"Yesssss!" screamed John. Both feet left the ground and he waved his arms at his father in the stand.

Dad gave a thumbs up. John was picked for the squad.

CHAPTER SEVEN

Grown-up Choices

"DAD," JOHN ASKED HIS FATHER ONE DAY, "which should I choose? Football or law?"

"I thought you liked cricket, like me," his dad replied in surprise. "You play a really good game, you know. You should become a cricketer."

"No, Dad," said John. "You know I prefer football."

"Listen to me, young man. I don't want you playing football. Cricket is better. Or you would be better off becoming a doctor."

John was confused. He didn't want to argue with his dad. But he also knew that he didn't want to be a

doctor or a cricketer. He loved football. Time passed and then one weekend, one of the top footballers he most admired was badly injured during a match. That player's career had ended at the age of only twenty-five. And he wasn't the only one...

John's 'O' and 'A' Level grades were excellent and one of his teachers encouraged him to apply to Oxford University. He was called for an interview.

"Dad, I've got an interview to study law at Oxford. Brilliant, isn't it? Not many in my year even got an interview. Just think, Dad, Oxford!"

"Well done," his father replied, "but you should do medicine. It will be better for you."

"But Dad, I really want to do law."

"I'm not so sure about lawyers," his father replied. "Not sure if I trust them. Shady bunch."

John knew there was no point arguing.

He went for the interview at Hertford College, Oxford, completely confused and miserable. The interview went badly and he was not accepted.

His second choice was Keele University, where he was immediately offered a place to study law. John decided to take it. Slowly, his father began to get used to the idea that his son was going to be a lawyer.

CHAPTER EIGHT

University Days

LIKE SO MANY YOUNG PEOPLE, John found that living away from home for the first time was wonderful. He loved being at university. He loved the freedom of going out and coming in without anyone checking up on him.

His first experiment with cooking was dreadful. He was so hungry he ate what he had made anyway and felt quite ill.

"You look so thin, my dear," said his mother on his first visit home.

"Thin! The boy is a bag of bones," said his father.

"Going to university is the best thing I've ever done," said John, "but I miss your cooking Mum."

That first weekend home, his mother made him all his favourite meals: rice and peas, macaroni pie, and Caribbean chicken.

On Sunday night, he headed back up north with a rucksack stuffed full of food. Soon after, he taught himself to cook.

Life at university got better and better. It was there that he found his Christian faith and made life-long friends.

He really enjoyed studying law. He watched courtroom dramas on TV and dreamed of the day when he, too, would be a barrister, fighting for his clients and winning cases.

Whenever he could, John sat at the back of the local courthouse. He listened closely to the evidence and tried to work out whether witnesses were telling the truth or not. He tried to guess if the jury would find the accused 'guilty' or 'not guilty'.

He enjoyed the sense of drama in the court. He loved watching

the judge in his wig, the lawyers, the jury, the victims, the accused… everybody.

"It's better than the movies!" he told his friends.

Sometimes, though, John felt quite uncomfortable, especially when he looked at the faces of some of the people on trial.

"How would I feel, sending someone to jail for the rest of their life?" he asked himself. "Could I ever fight for someone accused of cold-blooded murder? How would I feel if I made an awful mistake and someone innocent went to jail! Winning cases would be great, but what about losing!"

There was a lot to think about.

Chapter Nine
A Captive Audience

John graduated from Keele University in 1978 with an Honours Degree in Law and English Literature.

In his final year at University he won the Gray's Inn Advocacy Prize – a top prize open to law students across the world. This meant that John was able to get a good job. He was appointed a junior barrister in the Temple, London. He enjoyed being a lawyer. His chambers, as a barrister's office is called, was a famous place to work. One of the lawyers working there, called John Mortimer, had written the series of books, *Rumpole of the Bailey*. The books were also made into a popular television series.

Despite his best efforts, John seemed to get very little work and had difficulty earning a decent salary. Sadly, he came to realise that some of the seniors did not like black people and were making it difficult for him to get work. There was nothing to do but move to another chambers.

"I'll go back to Birmingham," he said to himself one day. In a matter of months he had found another chambers. It was better and he was happy.

He was even happier when his girlfriend, Kathie, agreed to be his wife. They had a most beautiful summer church wedding.

Then tragedy struck. His father fell ill and died. John was glad he could comfort his mother at this time.

John's father had not had an easy life growing up in Jamaica. He was the seventh in a family of eight children. He had often told John stories of how strict his own father (John's grandfather) had been.

The problem for John was that John's father had repeated this strict behaviour with him. He had never praised John for his successes.

Several times John had overheard his father saying to his friends at the cricket club, "He's a good lad, my son. And he's clever too!" But it wasn't the same. John wanted his dad to say it to him.

He would have liked his father to show him how proud he was of his school work and his exam results.

Then, John and Kathie had a beautiful, bouncing, baby daughter, Laura. They looked forward to having more.

"I will always praise my children for the good things they have done. Always," John vowed.

Chapter Ten
Going into Politics

"I LIKE MY WORK, but I'm worried about some of the old fashioned laws still being used," John told his friend Michael as they sat drinking coffee in a café used regularly by lawyers.

"I would like to be involved in changing things. I believe that yesterday in court, the wrong man went to prison. Today, someone was charged under a law made in the sixteenth century."

"You'll have to become a politician then," Michael replied. "You shouldn't have a problem though. The political parties are always on the look out for bright, professional people like you, especially given your skill as a lawyer."

John studied the political parties closely. He chose to join the Conservatives. John was determined to make the party more open to other black people. He was soon selected to fight a local council seat in Solihull, Birmingham. He had to knock on doors and convince complete strangers to vote for him.

He pressed the bell of the first house with butterflies in his stomach.

"Hello, I'm John Taylor your local Conservative candidate," he told the old woman who opened the door. "I hope I can rely on your vote at the election."

"I always vote for your party," she replied.

The butterflies in his stomach calmed down a little bit. "I hope they're all like this," he thought.

He was about to walk away, when she blurted out, "But…"

John's butterflies came back.

"I'm worried about how high the local rates are. What are you going to do about that?"

"We are determined to bring rates down," John told her confidently.

"And," she went on, "we also need a zebra crossing here. It's dangerous for the children and the old people like myself."

John smiled. He thought of his own mother and hoped he would win, so that he could help people like her.

He rang the next bell.

A large man came to the door. "Whaddya want?"

"Hello, I'm John Taylor your local Conservative candidate…"

"No. Go away. I never vote for you lot. You're a load of snobs."

He walked for miles and knocked on many doors.

On election day at the town hall, there was a great

buzz of activity. The counting of votes seemed to take forever. Eventually the announcement came.

"The elected member for St. Alphege, Solihull, is… JOHN TAYLOR!"

A tremendous roar of support rose from his party members and nearly lifted him off his feet. He had won! John served on the Council for four years, from 1986 to 1990.

CHAPTER ELEVEN
1992 and All That

ALTHOUGH WORKING AS A COUNCILLOR was rewarding, John soon wanted to move on. He wanted to get into Parliament.

"I want to be an MP," John told his mother.

Mrs Taylor was very proud of her son, but she was concerned.

"Are you sure, son?" she asked. "Aren't you busy enough? You'll have so much attention heaped on you. TV, newspapers, all ready to dish the dirt."

"Yes, Mum. I'm sure – but they won't find any!"

"John," said his mum, "look at all the things you already do: you're a Barrister at Law, a Borough Councillor, you work with the Department of Trade and Industry Think Tank. Then there's your work with the Home Office and the North Thames Regional Health Authority. Isn't that enough? And, John, don't forget your articles for the *Sunday Times*, *Daily Express* and the *Daily Telegraph*!"

But John was adamant.

The 1992 general election was in sight and he wanted to be in that battle.

CHAPTER TWELVE

Standing for Parliament

CAMPAIGNING FOR A SEAT IN PARLIAMENT in a general election was far more difficult than in a local council election. The number of people involved was far, far greater. Newspaper and television reporters were always around, looking for a story. John Taylor knew that he would become a very public figure.

He had no problems at all being selected as a Conservative Parliamentary candidate. However, when the day arrived for John and his wife, Kathie, to face the local Conservative party in Cheltenham, where he was going to be campaigning for election to Parliament, there was trouble.

Hundreds of people filled the huge hall as the meeting began.

"We don't want you here. Go away!"

a shrill, rasping voice immediately whipped across the room.

"We don't want somebody black representing us," another voice followed.

These voices belonged to members of his own chosen party – the Conservatives! John was horrified. He had hoped to be judged – like his hero Martin Luther King – not by the colour of his skin, but by the content of his character.

But there were other voices in the room that spoke in his favour. Many people thought he was the best person to represent the local party at the election and in the end he was chosen. He had won the first stage of his battle.

The national newspapers were now desperate for an interview. Journalists chased him everywhere. John's face appeared in most newspapers and on all the television channels. He carried on campaigning bravely to get into Parliament.

He gave interviews. He worked long hours. He let no opportunity pass to speak to the local people in Cheltenham and on their behalf.

He had thousands of letters of support, but he also faced heckling, ignorance and abuse. At home he had love and support from his family. His Christian faith and his family would always be more important than politics. And of course, there was football. He still supported Aston Villa and watched as many matches as he could.

In the middle of all this, his mother suffered a serious stroke. She had to be rushed to hospital, but luckily she survived.

Chapter Thirteen

Election Day

John carried on fighting. His phone rang non-stop. Many people wanted him to lash out at the racists.

He didn't. John was determined not to sink to the racists' level. The number of letters of support he received grew daily. People were impressed by his behaviour. They found him to be clever and well mannered. Just the sort of person, they said in their letters, they would like to have as their Member of Parliament. John Major, the then Prime Minister, also spoke in his favour.

Election day finally came. John was hoarse from speaking so much. He was weary and tense with anxiety. Journalists had come from all over the world. There were banks of television cameras. The count was on.

John became very optimistic as the count neared the end. His supporters stood close by, ready to celebrate a victory…

LORD TAYLOR OF WARWICK

CHAPTER FOURTEEN

Becoming a Lord

HE LOST. The winner was punching the air with excitement, but John went home that night a deeply disappointed man. He had lost by only a narrow margin and his family and close friends gathered around and reminded him of what he had achieved.

"Over 27,000 people voted for you," his wife said. "They all thought you were the best man for the job!"

John returned to his work as a lawyer. Then one day, he answered what he believed to be an ordinary telephone call. That call was far from ordinary.

"Hello, is that John Taylor?" a voice asked.

"Yes, speaking," replied John.

"I am calling on behalf of the Prime Minister, John Major. He wants you to become a Lord."

John could not believe his ears. He was being recognised for all the work he had done over the years. All his contributions to the people and the country had been noticed and rewarded. He called his family with the news. They were overjoyed.

"What does this mean, John?" his mother asked.

"Being a Lord is a job. We have to look at the laws that the Members of Parliament pass and try to improve them if necessary. Exactly what I always wanted to do!" John told her. "We also help charities and other groups understand how these laws affect them."

"I'm so happy for you, son," said his mother. "What a long road we've travelled together. What a blessing."

A journalist from a leading newspaper called Lord John Taylor of Warwick for an interview.

"My Lord," he said, "now that you have achieved one of the highest offices in the land, have you any other goals?"

John knew the answer without having to think. He replied, "I would still love to play football for England!"

On 21 September 1999, that dream came true...

John played in the England Parliamentary Football XI against the Hungarian Parliamentary XI at Upton Park, West Ham's stadium.

"I'm honoured to be allowed to wear the full England kit," said John, as he swapped his baronial robes for the white shirt.

APPENDIX

Lord Taylor's Achievements

LAW
1978 Barrister-at-Law; BA (Hons) Law Degree; Gray's Inn Advocacy Award winner
1997 Appointed by Lord Chancellor as Judge, sitting part-time
1999 Honorary Doctorate in Law, LLD, Warwick University

CORPORATE
1993– Chairman, Warwick Consulting International Ltd
1998 Vice President, National Small Business Bureau; Vice President, British Board of Film Classification
1998 Keynote Speaker, National BMBA Business Conference, Detroit, USA

MEDIA
TV and Radio Presenter, *Crime Stalker*, Carlton TV; *Talk About*, BBC1; *The John Taylor Programme*, BBC Radio2; *Powerhouse*, Channel 4

POLITICS
1986–90 Solihull Borough Councillor
1990–91 Special Adviser to the Home Secretary and Ministers of State
1992 Parliamentary Candidate for Cheltenham
1996 Life Peerage
1997 Introduced and carried through the Criminal Evidence Amendment Act 1997
1998 Keynote Speaker, 50th Human Rights Conference, Moscow, Russia

COMMUNITY
1992–4 Non Executive Director, North West Thames Regional
   Health Authority
Former Warwickshire County Colts Cricketer; County Area
   Rugby, Athletics; England International Parliamentary
   Soccer XI; Former Aston Villa F.C. Youth Team
Committee member, Royal Television Society; Variety Club
   Children's Charity; Radio Academy; Patron, Parents for
   Children Charity; Patron, Kidscape
Committee member, SCAR (Sickle Cell Anaemia Relief)
President, African Caribbean Westminster Initiative Business
   Association
President, West Indian Senior Citizens' Association
President, Ilford Town Football Club
1999 Director, The Warwick Leadership Foundation

Lord Taylor is married to Lady Katherine, a doctor. They have two daughters and a son.

website: www.lordtaylor.org